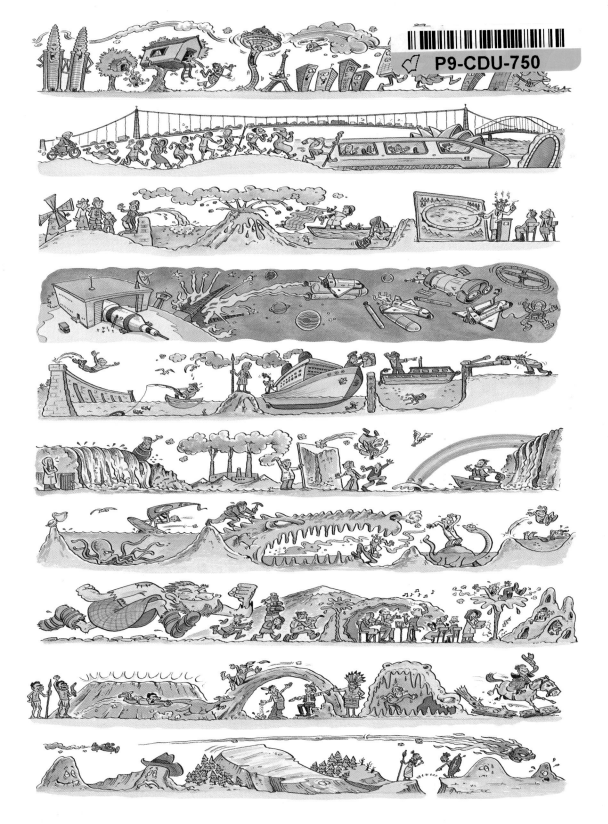

100

things you should know about

WORLD
WONDERS

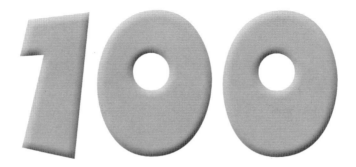

100

things you should know about

WORLD
WONDERS

Adam Hibbert

Consultant: Philip Steele

Miles Kelly
PUBLISHING

First published in 2005 by
Miles Kelly Publishing Ltd
Bardfield Centre, Great Bardfield, Essex, CM7 4SL

2 4 6 8 10 9 7 5 3 1

Publishing Director: Anne Marshall
Editor: Belinda Gallagher
Editorial Assistant: Lisa Clayden
Designer: John Christopher, White Design
Copy Editor: Sarah Ridley
Proofreader: Hayley Kerr
Indexer: Jane Parker

ISBN 1-84236-588-6

Printed in China

British Library Cataloguing-in-Publication Data
A catalogue record for this book is available from the British Library

ACKNOWLEDGEMENTS

The publishers would like to thank the following artists who
have contributed to this book:

Lisa Alderson
Syd Brak
Kuo Kang Chen
Peter Dennis
Richard Draper
Nicholas Forder
Mike Foster/Maltings Partnership
Luigi Galante
Alan Hancock

John James
Alessandro Menchi
Kevin Maddison
Janos Marffy
Terry Riley
Martin Sanders
Rudi Vizi
Steve Weston
John Woodcock

Cartoons by Mark Davis at Mackerel

www.mileskelly.net
info@mileskelly.net

Contents

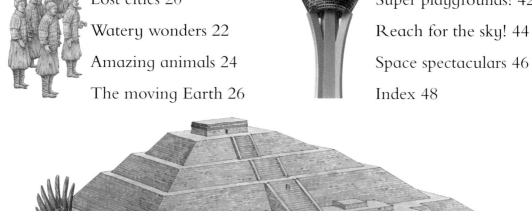

Wonder of Greece

1 **A goddess once lived in a temple in Greece.**
The Parthenon was a temple built to honour the goddess Athena. It is still one of the best examples of ancient Greek architecture. The temple was built from beautiful white marble. It contained a vast sculpture of the goddess Athena, which would have amazed and terrified visitors. Remains of the temple still stand today on the Acropolis, a hill overlooking the city of Athens.

▶ The temple complex at the Acropolis was dotted with statues and smaller temples, as well as housing the main temple, the Parthenon. Inside the Parthenon was a sculpture of Athena over 12 metres tall, made of gold and ivory.

Parthenon, home of Athena

Ancient world wonders

2 **The Romans built a massive stadium for deadly duels.** The Colosseum was a giant stone stadium that held crowds of 50,000 people. Emperors and other rich Romans paid for 'games' including gladiator battles and prisoner fights with wild beasts. The arena could be flooded for miniature naval battles between gladiator armies.

3 The great lighthouse at Alexandria, Egypt, was more than 100 metres tall, with a blazing fire at the top. It stood for 1500 years until it was destroyed by an earthquake. The lighthouse was built during the reign of pharaoh Ptolemy II (283–246BC) and became known as one of the seven wonders of the ancient world.

▼ The Colosseum was opened by the emperor Titus in AD80. It was so well designed that huge crowds could get in and out of the building in minutes.

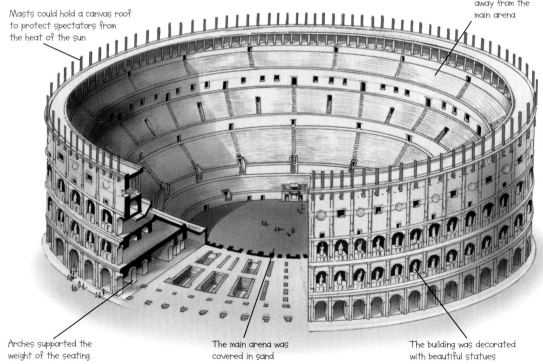

Masts could hold a canvas roof to protect spectators from the heat of the sun

Less wealthy people had to sit further away from the main arena

Arches supported the weight of the seating

The main arena was covered in sand

The building was decorated with beautiful statues

◄ The Great Sphinx was carved from stone over 4500 years ago.

6 **The ancient Greek Temple of Artemis was hidden under a swamp.** The archaeologist John Wood discovered it in the 19th century. The temple was built over the site of two earlier shrines at Ephesus, Asia Minor. It was dedicated to the goddess Artemis. Archaeologists are still finding the offerings of pilgrims from across the Greek world.

4 **A giant man–lion protects the pyramids.** The Great Sphinx is a huge statue of a half-man, half-lion that guards the pyramids at Giza, Egypt. It probably shows the dead king Khafre as a man with the fearsome power of a lion. The Sphinx is so old that sand blowing in the wind has rubbed away detail of the lion's body and parts of Khafre's face.

▲ The Temple of Artemis was famous for its beautiful marble decoration.

5 **The Hanging Gardens didn't really hang.** Greeks were amazed by the city of Babylon, in modern Iraq. They found a fantastic garden with terraces on different levels, covered by spectacular plants. It was said that a Babylonian king had it built to remind his queen, who was from a mountain region, of her childhood.

▶ To water The Hanging Gardens, slaves worked in shifts, lifting water from the Euphrates River.

7 **Alexandria's famous library was burnt to cinders.** Arts, maths and sciences were developed more in Alexandria, Egypt, than anywhere else in the ancient world. Most of the knowledge recorded in the library was lost when Christians burnt it to the ground in the year AD391.

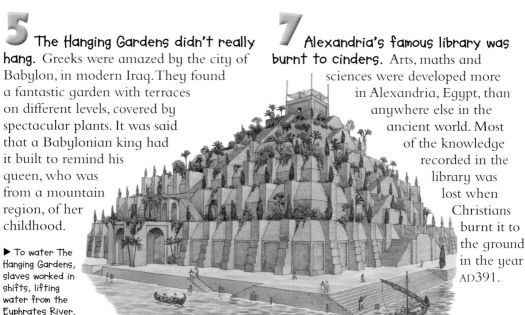

The amazing Americas

◀ The mountain city of Machu Picchu was a forgotten marvel, lost for 400 years.

8 **The Egyptians weren't the only ones to build pyramids.** Some pyramid-builders lived in Central and South America. Instead of using them as tombs, the Incas, the Maya and the Aztecs used their pyramids as temples. Without modern technology, a pyramid shape is the safest one to use for big buildings.

9 **The Incas built a mountaintop city.** Machu Picchu was a city high in the Andes Mountains, with gardens, a temple and a fortress. The city was built from large, interlocking stones and watered by a spring at the top of the mountain. It was so well-hidden, Spanish invaders never found it. In 1911, the city was rediscovered by American explorer Hiram Bingham.

10 **Not all monuments are built of stone.** The Nazca people scratched huge patterns and pictures into the stony deserts of Peru, which are only properly visible from the air. Some of the patterns are simple squares and triangles, and some are line drawings of animals, such as a spider and a monkey. No one knows for certain what they were for.

11 **Chan Chan was an amazing city built of mud bricks (adobe).** The Chimú were farming people who became wealthy and created a small empire in Peru. The richest Chimú families built compounds in Chan Chan. Each compound contained gardens, pyramids and warehouses. They were decorated with beautiful carvings and patterns.

12 **Teotihuacán was the greatest city in the New World.** Before Europeans arrived in the Americas, this civilization rose and fell in Mexico. It left a huge city, with two great pyramids dedicated to the Sun and Moon, and a vast temple for Quetzalcóatl, the feathered snake god.

▼ The Moon Pyramid of Teotihuacán contains the remains of six smaller buildings.

13 **The Aztecs farmed on a lake.** After the Aztecs founded their capital city on an island in a lake, their society began to grow. They made the island bigger by building flat platforms of reed and coating them with mud from the lake bottom. Then they grew crops and raised animals on the platforms.

African marvels

14 **Nigeria was a centre of metalwork wonders.** The Benin Empire was founded in the 11th century AD. It was famous for its brass sculptures. Benin City, the capital, survived until 1897, when the British destroyed it, taking thousands of statues.

◄ The brass sculptures of Benin, such as this head, were produced from the 1500s onwards.

15 **In Cameroon, the pyramids were made from bamboo.** Many different Africans came to the Bamileke region to settle. Some built the pyramid roofs of their houses out of long bamboo stalks, then hoisted them into the air and placed the walls underneath. They were up to 10 metres tall.

16 **Zimbabwe was a great stone city.** All through the Middle Ages, a powerful African nation had its centre at Great Zimbabwe. Around a fortified stone compound with its impressive tower, the stone buildings covered the valley and a nearby hilltop. The Karanga people used the local gold to trade with partners as far away as China.

◄ Around this stone compound in Zimbabwe, the House of the Great Woman, rose a great city of 20,000 Africans.

17 **Mali's mosque looks like a giant sandcastle.**
Djenne is home to an amazing mosque. It is built by
hand from mud and mud bricks, with wooden steps
poking through the surface to help builders
scramble up and down. Djenne was once
an important trading post and centre
of Muslim thought. The
mosque is repaired
with fresh mud each
spring, in a huge
festival involving
the whole
community.

▼ The Great Mosque of
Djenne is 100 years old.
It stands where great
mosques have stood
for 800 years.

18 **St George's Church in Ethiopia
is made from one solid rock.** In about
AD1200, King Lalibela started a programme
of church-building. The builders dug a deep
trench around a massive rock, carved it into
the shape of a cross and then hollowed it out
to make the church.

19 **Dogon houses were shaped like
people.** The Dogon tribe of Mali built
their houses to represent a person lying on
the floor – with a fireplace for a head, store
rooms for arms, a workroom for the belly
and stables in the place of legs.

AFRICAN QUIZ
1. The Benin Empire was
famous for (a) wooden carvings
or (b) brass sculptures?
2. Pyramids in Cameroon
were built with (a) bamboo
or (b) grass?
3. The Karanga people traded
with (a) gold or (b) silver?
4. The Great Mosque of
Djenne is (a) 50 years or
(b) 100 years old?

Answers:
1b 2a 3a 4b

Temple lands

20 **King Kashyapa ruled from inside a lion.** The Sri Lankan king's mountain fortress was known as Sigiriya, or Lion's Mouth, because it could only be reached by climbing through well-guarded gates, carved in the shape of a lion's gaping jaw. His fortress was on a small plateau made by an ancient volcano, 180 metres above the plain below.

▲ The Lion's Mouth gate to Sigiriya has gone, but the two giant lion's paws remain.

21 **The city of Pagan had 4000 Buddhist shrines.** Pagan was once the capital of Burma (modern-day Myanmar) in Southeast Asia. In the city's richest era, from around 1060 to 1280, thousands of Buddhist shrines and monuments were built. The city has since disappeared, but 2000 shrines can still be seen.

22 **Khajraho's 85 temples were lost for 500 years.** India's Chandela kings abandoned their Hindu temple city of Khajraho for the safety of hill forts during a chaotic period of India's history. Later Muslim rulers knew nothing of the Hindu shrines, so they survived unharmed until they were rediscovered in 1838 by a British army officer.

I DON'T BELIEVE IT!

We still can't crack the code of writings on 4000-year-old tablets from the Harappa Empire in India.

24 **A temple in Java swallowed a hill!** Buddhists built one huge shrine at Borobudur, by shaping a small hill and casing it with stone blocks. They added some amazing sculpture. Since 1972 all 800,000 stones have been taken away, cleaned and replaced.

◄ The Borobudur 'hill' temple of Java is home to 2000 carvings, 72 shrines and 500 Buddhas.

23 **Farmers built staircases on mountains.** Water-loving rice plants can't grow on steep hills, but East Asian farmers found ways to use their mountain landscape. They made stepped terraces which could hold muddy pools for their crops. Whole mountains were transformed.

▼ The moat around Angkor Wat measures 6 kilometres. It is as wide as three jumbo jets.

25 **Angkor Wat was the biggest temple ever built.** The Khmer kingdom in Cambodia was believed to be ruled by god-kings. Their capital at Angkor contained a huge complex of temple buildings, with artificial lakes, moats and long boundary walls covered in carvings. The biggest temple, Angkor Wat, was saved from the jungle by Buddhist monks after the Khmer kingdom collapsed.

Splendours of the East

26 **One wall is 6400 kilometres long.** Chinese civilization was based on farming, and the young Chinese nation was often raided by nomads from the North. From 214BC onwards, China built a stone wall along the border to keep its nuisance neighbours out. The wall was 9 metres high, with watchtowers and a walkway along the top for the guards.

▲ The Great Wall of China includes many walls built by different emperors over several centuries. The Wall was originally dotted with watchtowers.

▼ Thousands of clay soldiers were buried with Emperor Qin Shi Huangdi to make him mighty in heaven.

27 **There is a city inside the city of Beijing.** The Emperor of China once lived inside his own city, with hundreds of buildings and 9000 rooms, all contained within 16 kilometres of high walls. It was known as the Forbidden City because no one was allowed to enter without a special invitation from the Emperor's court. It is now a museum.

28 **An emperor was buried with clay soldiers.** According to Chinese tradition, the dead should be buried or cremated with items that would be useful to them in heaven. Normally this means a few handfuls of money. But the first emperor of China, Qin Shi Huangdi, was buried with 7000 life-size clay soldiers.

29
Japanese tombs were shaped like keyholes. Japan became a powerful country in the Yamato era, between AD250 and 500. The Yamato nobles were buried in huge tombs, which are keyhole-shaped when seen from above. It took 800,000 people to build Emperor Nintoku's tomb.

31
Koreans were early astronomers. The ancient Silla kingdom of Korea was ruled by Queen Sondok, in the 7th century. She had an observatory built for studying the stars. The observatory still stands today, although it is not used.

30
A giant Buddha sits in the world's biggest wooden building. The wooden Todai-ji Temple in Japan is 57 metres long, 50 metres wide and 47 metres high, but used to be even bigger. For almost 1500 years it has been the home of a giant bronze Buddha statue, made from 130 tonnes of bronze and leafed in 130 kilograms of gold.

▶ The Todai-ji Buddha promises peace after conflict. Each finger is over one metre long.

Mighty monuments

32 **Stone giants on Easter Island weigh as much as 1000 men.** Giant stone statues, called *moai*, frightened the first European visitors to Easter Island in the Pacific Ocean. The biggest of the 600 figures weighs at least 75 tonnes, not including its 11-tonne hat, called a *pukao*. Carved from single blocks of stone, the statues were moved great distances before being placed to mark tombs. The eyes were made of coral.

◄ The mysterious giant heads on Easter Island have frightened sailors for hundreds of years.

33 **Ancient Britons built a huge stone circle.** Stonehenge in England was made from giant stones, some of which were brought 385 kilometres from a quarry in Wales. They were arranged so that the sun shone into the entranceway on the morning of the longest day of summer – the summer solstice. The solstice was the most important festival day for farmers. People prayed that crops would grow well before harvesting.

► Stonehenge was built 4000 years ago.

34 **One giant mound in Britain is a total mystery.** The same ancient Britons who built Stonehenge also built a mysterious hill. Silbury Hill is near Avebury, another stone circle, but its purpose is unknown. It is 40 metres tall and 30 metres across at the top. There is no sign of a tomb inside.

35 **Some religious parades may have lasted one kilometre or more.** Holy men of northern France may have walked the long, stone avenue at Carnac, Brittany, every sunrise and sunset. Prehistoric religious carvings on some of the stones there were later added to with Roman graffiti and Christian symbols.

STONE CRAZY!

Large stone structures built by prehistoric people are called megaliths. The people who made them had no metal tools — some megaliths were carved from blocks of stone using handheld stone chisels. But to carve stone with a stone, you have to know which stone is toughest. Try placing these stones in order of hardness:

a. Marble b. Granite
c. Diamond d. Limestone
e. Quartz

Answers:
c e b a d

36 **Temples on the island of Malta have stood for 5000 years.** The oldest buildings in the world are in Malta. Ancient farmers worshipped goddesses of fertility and built temples out of limestone for religious rituals. The temples housed small statues of an 'earth mother' goddess.

Lost cities

37 Ancient cities have been swallowed by the sea. The sea level in the Mediterranean has changed since cities began to be built around it. The coastline of Lebanon is dotted with underwater cities, such as Yarmuta, which were abandoned as the sea rose. The Black Sea coastline was pushed back at a speed of over one kilometre a day when the Mediterranean began to pour in, 7500 years ago.

▲ According to legend, the island of Atlantis sunk beneath the sea. Scientists now think that stories about Atlantis could relate to the Greek island of Thira, which was destroyed by volcanic eruptions in 1470BC.

38 The island of Atlantis was lost in legend. The ancient Greeks told stories of an island in the Atlantic Ocean that once sent armies to rule the Mediterranean. But legend has it that island sank below the waves after earthquake damage.

I DON'T BELIEVE IT!

There are three Roman columns near Naples in Italy that have been nibbled by shellfish. This proves they were underwater at some point. Volcanic activity can push or drop the coastline by several metres.

39 Cleopatra's palace lies below fishing boats. After the Romans took over Alexandria in Egypt around 100BC, the city became less important. Alexandrians moved their city inland, away from the rising sea. The old city is now being found under the waters of the harbour.

40 **An Egyptian city appeared in America.** A huge Egyptian sphinx was uncovered not far from El Paso, Texas, in 1999. But it turned out not to be real. It was a set for a film, *The Ten Commandments*. It had been hidden by Cecil B. de Mille in 1923 to keep details of the film secret before it was released.

41 **There may be a city half a kilometre under the sea near Cuba.** Scientists have scanned the seabed of an area, Cabo de San Antonio, off the coast of Cuba. They have seen regular-shaped structures 600 metres down, but cannot tell if the street and house shapes are man-made or something natural, such as coral.

42 **Japan's undersea pyramid may be a freak of nature.** Off the southernmost island of Japan, close to Taiwan, a stone mound has been discovered by divers, with what could be steps, carvings and a roadway. It looks like an Inca temple, but geologists say that all the odd features could be explained by the effect of waves smashing into the rock.

▲ This underwater 'pyramid' off the coast of Yonaguni Island, Japan, could be the oldest man-made structure ever found.

Watery wonders

43 **Undersea vents feed spooky creatures.** Almost all life on Earth depends on the Sun to provide energy. But undersea vents feed some very strange-looking life forms. They give off clouds of hot water that contain minerals. These feed tiny plants and animals, which are eaten by tube worms and giant clams, a kind of shellfish.

44 **The deepest place in the sea is the Mariana Trench.** It marks the spot where the huge Pacific plate plunges beneath the continental plate of East Asia. It is 2500 kilometres long, and some parts are over 11 kilometres below sea level.

Rat tail fish

Giant clams

I DON'T BELIEVE IT!

Before ships had engines, the oceans were a quieter place for animals to live. Whales could hear their mates calling from the other side of the world!

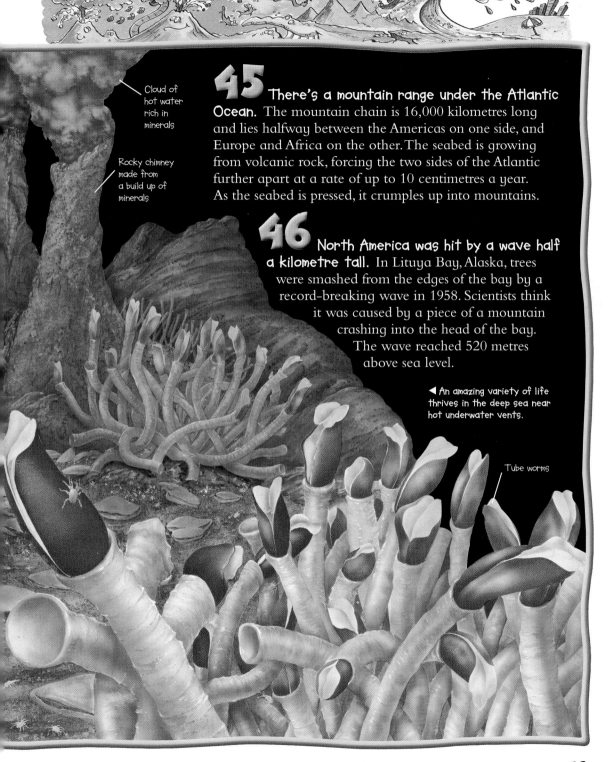

Cloud of hot water rich in minerals

Rocky chimney made from a build up of minerals

45 There's a mountain range under the Atlantic Ocean.

The mountain chain is 16,000 kilometres long and lies halfway between the Americas on one side, and Europe and Africa on the other. The seabed is growing from volcanic rock, forcing the two sides of the Atlantic further apart at a rate of up to 10 centimetres a year. As the seabed is pressed, it crumples up into mountains.

46 North America was hit by a wave half a kilometre tall.

In Lituya Bay, Alaska, trees were smashed from the edges of the bay by a record-breaking wave in 1958. Scientists think it was caused by a piece of a mountain crashing into the head of the bay. The wave reached 520 metres above sea level.

◀ An amazing variety of life thrives in the deep sea near hot underwater vents.

Tube worms

Amazing animals

47 **A monarch butterfly flies 3000 kilometres.** Monarch butterflies in North America swarm together for a winter holiday. They fly from colder northern areas down to the forests of southern California and Mexico. In spring they return some of the way, lay eggs and die. Their young continue the trip north for summer.

▲ Monarch butterflies live in several parts of the world, but the American species travels furthest.

48 On Christmas Island in the Indian Ocean, the ground turns red twice a year. Red forest-living crabs migrate in huge swarms to the seashore, where their eggs are laid all at once. Then their tiny young return after a few months as larvae.

▲ Red crabs have to dip in the sea after their long walk, to save themselves from drying out.

▶ This coral polyp has built itself a cup of limestone, making a shelter like a snail's shell.

49 Tiny corals build a home you can see from space. The Great Barrier Reef runs up the northeast coast of Australia for 2000 kilometres. It is built and renewed by billions of tiny coral polyps, less than one centimetre across. Over a period of 20 million years, these tiny animals have created a world wonder that can be seen from space.

coral polyp

50 Termite cities have air conditioning. Termite nests are often out of sight, but some poke up through the soil to form strange mounds. In northern Australia, these nests line up north to south. Scientists think the termites use the Sun's energy to circulate cool air within the nest.

I DON'T BELIEVE IT!

Sea creatures often produce millions of eggs, because so many will be eaten by hungry predators.

▶ Termite mounds are built to keep the right mix of air and moisture in the nest below.

The moving Earth

51 The rocks at the bottom of the Grand Canyon are two billion years old. The Colorado River in the United States has worn away tonnes of rock, creating a huge canyon that extends for 446 kilometres. In places, the canyon is 1.6 kilometres deep and 29 kilometres wide.

52 A meteorite left a hole in Arizona. Barringer Crater in the United States is one kilometre across and 180 metres deep. Droplets of metal and glass can be found for up to 100 kilometres around the crater. They are the remains of a metal meteorite, which exploded on impact with Earth.

▼ A 300,000–tonne metal meteorite crashed into Arizona and exploded, about 50,000 years ago. It left this enormous crater in the earth.

53 The wind can make a mountain of sand. The Dune of Pilat on the French Atlantic coast has been created by wind and waves piling up sand from the bay over the last 200 years. The dune is 105 metres high, 500 metres wide and nearly 3 kilometres long. It is slowly creeping inland. A pine forest has been planted to try to slow it down.

◄ The Grand Canyon is one of the biggest wonders in the natural world. The colours of the rocks can be brilliant shades of red and brown, especially at sunset.

55 Africa is tearing in two along the Rift Valley. This giant tear – 4000 kilometres long, 100 kilometres wide and up to 2 kilometres deep, is forming as Africa and Asia slowly pull apart. The tear has allowed hot rock from below to force through in places, forming mountains such as Mount Kilimanjaro.

I DON'T BELIEVE IT!

Before it was dammed, the Colorado River carried 500,000 tonnes of sand and sediment a day – enough grit to cut through the toughest rock.

▼ It can take rock climbers four days to climb El Capitan.

54 Yosemite was carved by tonnes of ice. The Yosemite National Park, in the Sierra Nevada, United States, has some of the most amazing rocks in the world. El Capitan is a smooth block of granite rising almost one kilometre from the valley below. It was carved out of the landscape by a huge glacier that slid past like a giant sheet of sandpaper.

Outrageous rock!

56 **The rock of Uluru changes colour through the day.** The weird lump of rock lying stranded in Australia's outback is a sacred site for Aborigines. Once known as Ayers Rock, the reddish sandstone goes through amazing colour changes at sunrise and sunset. Grooves and holes worn by rain and sandstorms create a strange series of shadows that move across the stone.

57 **Rock can make a bridge.** American Indians believed that a rainbow had been turned to stone when they visited the Rainbow Bridge, 93 metres high and 85 metres long, in Utah, United States. The sandstone bridge can appear pink, red or lavender-coloured in sunlight.

▶ A walk around the base of Uluru covers almost 10 kilometres. The rock has lots of small caves, of which many are covered with Aboriginal paintings.

58 **Huge rooms can be carved from rock.** The caves at Sarawak, Malaysia, are gigantic. The Deer Cave is almost 100 metres wide, 100 metres high, and over 2 kilometres long! That's enough room for 20 full-size soccer pitches.

59 **Some rocks used to be trees.** Near Winslow, Arizona, the desert is covered with stone logs – fossils of giant trees that once grew there. The logs crystallized as they lay in mud, and were buried for millions of years. The crystals preserve details such as the growth rings of the tree trunks.

I DON'T BELIEVE IT!

There is a desert of white sand in New Mexico. The grains of sand are made from gypsum. Rare white lizards and mice have evolved to blend in with the white background.

Hot stuff!

60 **Volcanoes can make neat pavements.**
The Giant's Causeway in Ireland was formed
by a volcano's lava flow. It cooled slowly,
cracking from the surface downwards like
drying mud, to form six-sided stone 'logs'.
Irish tradition says that it was built
by a giant who wanted to make
a road to Scotland.

▼ Some of the stone columns
of Giant's Causeway are
up to 6 metres high.

61 **The Earth can spit
boiling water.** Wherever heat from
below ground makes contact with
water, you can find hot springs and geysers.
Whakarewarewa is New Zealand's most
spectacular hot spring area. Bubbling mud
and hot springs are overshadowed by
Pohutu, a geyser that hurls water and
steam 30 metres into the air.

MAKE A GEYSER
You can create a safe
geyser by releasing all the
bubbles in a bottle of fizzy
water at once. Standing
outside, give the
bottle a vigorous
shake and undo
the cap. There
she blows!

63 **When volcanoes die, they can leave houses behind.** The Urgup Cones in Turkey are all that is left of small volcanoes. Their outer layers have worn away, exposing solid lava cones that once filled the volcanoes' inner chambers. They have been carved out to make houses.

64 **You can enjoy a concert in a lava bubble.** As lava flows from a volcano, it cools from the outside, forming hard rock while the centre remains liquid. Sometimes this leaves a cave or tube inside the rock. At Cueva de los Verdes, in the Canary Islands, caves like these have been converted to make a concert hall.

▼ Mount Fuji is a volcano, which last erupted in 1707. It is visible from Tokyo, over 100 kilometres away.

▲ Houses carved from the Urgup Cones can be cool in summer and warm in winter.

62 **Pilgrims visit the volcano of Fuji.** Mount Fuji is Japan's biggest mountain – the result of thousands of eruptions of ash and lava. The shrines that circle the lip of the volcano's crater are home to young trainee priests in the Shinto religion.

Fantastic lakes

65 **Lakes can be found in the strangest places.** Crater Lake in Oregon is a beautiful, crystal-blue colour, but it's at the top of a mountain. When the old volcano, Mount Mazama, last erupted it left a bowl-shaped crater 10 kilometres across and almost 600 metres deep. Water from melted ice and snow has almost filled the bowl.

66 **You can visit an island on a lake on an island on a lake.** Lake Huron in North America has a large island, Manitoulin Island, the biggest island in any lake in the world. On Manitoulin is Lake Manitou, which is also big and has several smaller islands in it.

▼ America's deepest lake, Crater Lake, has a small volcano called Wizard Island in the middle. The lake is 589 metres at its greatest depth.

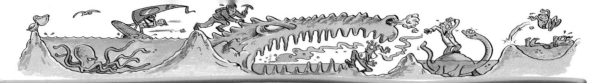

► There is so much salt in the water of the Dead Sea you can easily float.

67 **Some lakes are saltier than the sea.** The Dead Sea is a lake in the Middle East that is 400 metres below sea level. Water quickly evaporates from the lake's surface due to the hot climate, leaving behind minerals such as salt. The Dead Sea is about ten times saltier than seawater.

68 **There's a lake as old as the dinosaurs.** Lake Vostok, near the South Pole, has been cut off from the rest of the world for millions of years under a layer of Antarctic ice. Scientists are working out how to drill 4 kilometres down to the lake under the ice, without disturbing any life that may survive there.

69 **Lakes can be hidden away completely.** There is a lake in northeastern Namibia, Africa, which is deep underground inside its own cave. Dragon's Breath Cave supports life. With no sunlight, all the cave creatures rely on bat droppings as an energy source. As there is no light, the eyesight of the animals and fish that live there is extremely poor, and other senses such as touch and smell have become more developed.

I DON'T BELIEVE IT!

Lake Baikal in Russia is home to the world's only freshwater seals.

Wonderful waterfalls

70 Niagara Falls is moving upriver. The flowing water eats away at the rock below it, causing the lip of the falls to collapse. The waterfall then moves back a few metres. Niagara Falls has moved about one metre a year for the last 300 years. It has stabilized now because the Niagara River is redirected at night to hydroelectric power stations. Here, the water is used to provide electricity.

▲ Niagara Falls was formed about 12,000 years ago when a great ice sheet melted, causing the Niagara River to overflow. The Falls form part of the border between The United States and Canada.

71 One waterfall is nearly one kilometre tall.

Hidden away in the Venezuelan rainforest is a mountain with steep cliffs. The Angel Falls flows over the edge of one of these cliffs, and drops 979 metres through the air to the river below. It is the tallest waterfall in the world.

◀ Angel Falls is 15 times taller than Niagara Falls. It was discovered in 1933 by American, Jimmy Angel.

WATERFALL QUIZ
1. How far has Niagara Falls been moving back each year?
2. Where are the Iguaçu Falls?
3. How much taller is Angel Falls than Niagara Falls?

Answers:
1.One metre a year 2. Argentina 3. 15 times taller

▼ The Iguaçu Falls form part of the border between Argentina and Brazil.

72 The Iguaçu waterfall makes beautiful rainbows.

About 12,750 cubic metres of water pour over the lip of the Iguaçu Falls in Argentina every second. The waterfall is broken into separate flows by rocky outcrops along the lip, which is 4 kilometres long. It creates so much spray that there are often several rainbows at once.

Waterworks!

73 **The Akosombo Dam has made a lake bigger than a country.** Lake Volta is 8000 square kilometres, about three times bigger than the country of Luxembourg. The lake was created by damming the Volta River in 1965 to provide water for farming. The artificial lake is not just a reservoir. It also supplies Ghana with electricity, an inland fishing resource and a navigation system – giving shipping links between the northern end of the country and the coast.

WATERWORKS QUIZ

1. What river was dammed to make the Akosombo Dam?
2. Which canal links two oceans?
3. How long is the Suez Canal?
4. Where is the world's busiest port?
5. Where might you find a lock on a canal?

Answers:
1. Volta River 2. The Panama Canal 3. 100 kilometres 4. Rotterdam 5. Where a canal goes uphill or downhill

▼ The Akosombo Dam was built in the 1960s. Electricity made here supplies three countries and powers Ghana's industries, such as an aluminium factory.

74 One canal links two oceans.

The Panama Canal in Central America connects the Atlantic and Pacific Oceans. It was built to save ships a long detour. At just 65 kilometres long, it saves ships travelling from one side of the United States to the other – a huge 12,000-kilometre trip around South America.

75 You can ride a ship through a desert.

In 1869 a French company completed 11 years of engineering to create the 100 kilometre-long Suez Canal. It passes through Egypt, linking the Mediterranean Sea with the Red Sea. The Suez Canal saves ships a 7700-kilometre detour through dangerous seas.

▲ The Suez Canal was opened in 1869.

▲ Ships mainly travel through the Suez Canal in single–line traffic as the canal is quite narrow.

76 The Dutch can shut a door to stop the tide coming in.

Rotterdam is the world's busiest port. It is built on land reclaimed from the mouth of the Rhine River, and used to be at risk from storm surges in the North Sea. It now has two huge doors that can be shut against extreme high tides. Each door is about 300 metres – taller than the Eiffel Tower.

77 Some boats use lifts!

When a canal climbs a hill, locks are needed to raise or lower boats, one 'step' at a time. This is slow work on a big hill. Instead of a series of locks, some canals have a boat 'lift', which carries a section of the canal, complete with water and boat, from the bottom to the top, or back again.

Shaping our world

▼ Two large fishing ports on the Aral Sea have been left dry as the shoreline drew back.

78 **The Aral Sea is shrinking.**
A huge lake in central Asia called the Aral Sea was once 15 metres deeper and twice as big. Rivers supplying it were used to water fields instead. The Aral Sea began to shrink and became three times saltier than it had been before, killing all its fish. Islands across the middle of the Aral Sea have now joined up, breaking the water into two separate lakes.

79 Lava can be used to make an island bigger. Iceland sits on the mid-Atlantic volcanic ridge, where there is lots of volcanic activity. In 1973, the villagers on the island of Vestmannaeyjar, Iceland, fought off a lava flow by pumping sea water at it, diverting it into the sea. The lava formed a new harbour wall for their fishing port, and added 2 square kilometres to their island.

▲ The 1973 lava flow improved the shape of the harbour, giving better shelter to boats.

UPHILL FLOW!

If the Low Countries had no way to pump water out, they would soon flood again. Make this simple pump. Ask an adult to help you

You will need:
two plastic bowls   water   plastic tubing   chair

1. Place an empty bowl on the floor.
2. Place a bowl of water on a chair.
3. Put one end of the tube in the bowl of water.
4. Suck through the tube to start the water moving.
5. Place the other end of the tube in the empty bowl. Water will rise up the tube and start to flow into the empty bowl.

80 Some countries keep growing bigger. The Netherlands is one of the Low Countries of Europe. They are called 'low' because much of their coastal land is actually below sea level. A quarter of the Netherlands has been reclaimed from river estuaries and the sea by building a system of earth walls, and pumping out the water.

81 It took 14 years to carve a mountain. Mount Rushmore in South Dakota, United States, was sculpted by 400 people over 14 years to create four huge stone portraits of American leaders. The side of the mountain that receives most sunlight shows the four faces, each with eyes 4 metres across.

From A to B

82 **Akashi Kaikyo Bridge reaches 2 kilometres in one step.** Japan is made up of four big islands and hundreds of smaller ones. People used to have to catch a ferry to travel from one big island, Shikoku, to the main island, Honshu. The Akashi Kaikyo Bridge reaches across the 2 kilometres of sea separating the two islands, allowing people to travel easily and quickly. This is the longest span of a bridge anywhere in the world.

I DON'T BELIEVE IT!

Scotland's Forth Bridge is always being painted. It takes a team of painters three years to paint its 521-metre length. By the time they've finished they have to start again.

83 **The longest pilgrimage of all is the Hajj.** For six days in the Islamic calendar's last month of the year, Mecca is host to two million pilgrims. Muslims from all countries and backgrounds come together to walk around the Kaaba in Mecca's Great Mosque, Muslims' holiest point on Earth. They also perform religious ceremonies.

84 Trains can zoom at 150 kilometres an hour under the sea.

The Eurotunnel connects mainland Britain with northern France. The three tunnels – two railways and a service tunnel – run for 14.7 kilometres under the sea, and another 30 kilometres under solid ground. Trains carry foot passengers as well as motorists in their own cars.

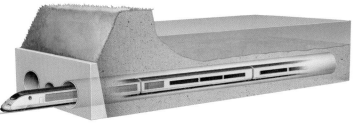

▲ The Eurotunnel linking Britain and France was first discussed in the 1700s – it was finished in 1995.

85 Sydney Harbour Bridge in Australia is the widest bridge in the world.

The bridge, completed in 1932, is almost 50 metres wide – carrying railway lines, traffic lanes, a cycle lane and a footpath.

◄ The Akashi Kaikyo Bridge uses enough cable to circle the Earth seven times.

▲ About 160,000 vehicles cross Sydney Harbour Bridge each day.

Super playgrounds!

86 The Skydome sports stadium in Toronto, Canada, is one of the world's biggest enclosed spaces. To show just how big, 46 full-size hot-air balloons were inflated inside it in 1992! The record-breaking sunroof slides open to reveal open sky in about 20 minutes.

87 Sydney Opera House was built twice. The weird shapes of the Sydney Opera House roof were so far ahead of their time that builders had to start work before the materials for the roof had even been invented. When the builders realized that the roof would be heavier than expected, they had to blow up the foundations and start again!

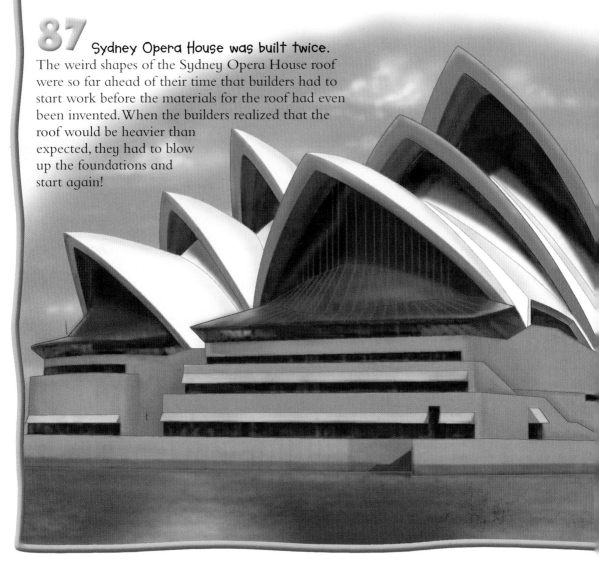

88

You can surf on a beach with a roof in Japan. The Seagaia Ocean Dome is an artificial indoor beach, with a sliding roof. Visitors can surf on artificial waves all year round. The 300 metre-long building is 100 metres from the actual coast.

89

In France there is a city of cinemas. Wonderful buildings are part of Futuroscope near Poitiers, France – a huge amusement park. Some of the cinemas there have screens that surround the viewer, and one plays a 3D film on a screen that's 15 metres high and 20 metres wide.

▼ The cinema screen inside Futuroscope's Kinemax building is the size of two tennis courts.

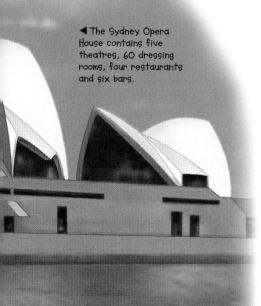

◄ The Sydney Opera House contains five theatres, 60 dressing rooms, four restaurants and six bars.

90

It takes an army to run Disney World. This amusement resort in Florida, United States, covers 120 square kilometres. It takes 45,000 guides, shop assistants, cleaners, cooks, medics and other staff to keep the park running. Visitors buy nine billion burgers and seven billion hotdogs each year!

I DON'T BELIEVE IT!

The white cladding on the shells of the Sydney Opera House is built from one million ceramic tiles!

Reach for the sky!

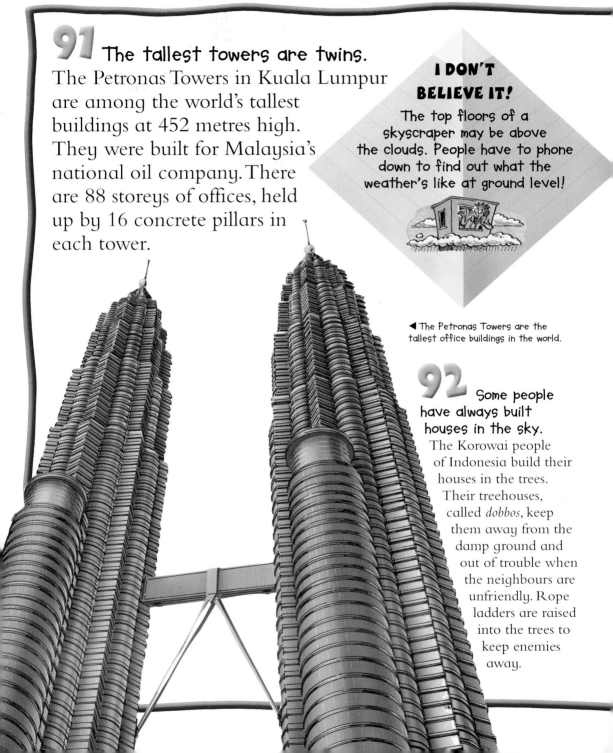

91 **The tallest towers are twins.** The Petronas Towers in Kuala Lumpur are among the world's tallest buildings at 452 metres high. They were built for Malaysia's national oil company. There are 88 storeys of offices, held up by 16 concrete pillars in each tower.

I DON'T BELIEVE IT!

The top floors of a skyscraper may be above the clouds. People have to phone down to find out what the weather's like at ground level!

◀ The Petronas Towers are the tallest office buildings in the world.

92 **Some people have always built houses in the sky.** The Korowai people of Indonesia build their houses in the trees. Their treehouses, called *dobbos*, keep them away from the damp ground and out of trouble when the neighbours are unfriendly. Rope ladders are raised into the trees to keep enemies away.

Rides at the top of the tower

93 You can rollercoast around one skyscraper.

In the heart of the desert in the southwestern United States, the city of Las Vegas has become America's main city of entertainment. Huge hotels and leisure buildings are overlooked by the Stratosphere Tower. There is a rollercoaster that travels around the tower at the top, 300 metres above the ground.

◀ The Big Shot and High Roller thrill rides travel around the top of the Stratosphere Tower.

94 Some skyscrapers dance in the wind.

Very tall skyscrapers are pushed around by the wind, causing the top floors to sway. This can make people feel sick. Some skyscrapers, such as the Citicorp Center in New York, USA, have weights at the top that are moved from side to side to make the building lean against the wind, cancelling out the effect.

95 The first skyscraper was built 120 years ago.

Chicago, a city in the midwestern United States, was once built of wood, but most of it burnt down in 1871. The old city was replaced with more modern buildings, including the ten-storey Home Insurance building, which was the first to use a metal frame.

▶ Chicago's Home Insurance building used lighter steel beams to build higher and faster.

Space spectaculars

96 **Rockets are built inside the tallest room in the world.** Some space rockets are over 100 metres tall. As they are made standing upright, they need a huge building in which to be made. NASA's Vehicle Assembly Building (VAB) in Florida, United States, is a 160 metres high, with doors that are 139 metres tall. The doors are bigger than a football pitch.

97 **There are four main parts to a space shuttle.** Each part is designed to help with a certain part of the journey. The shuttle has its own engines, but also straps on a fuel tank and two booster rockets to help it into space.

◀ NASA moves shuttles from the VAB on crawlers – trucks that weigh 2700 tonnes each.

98 The Hubble Telescope wears specs.

With shuttle trips, we can now repair broken satellites in space, or pick them up and bring them home for a service. The Hubble Telescope needed to be fitted with electronic spectacles before it could begin sending home its amazing views of deep space.

99 You can stay in space for a year.

The International Space Station (ISS) lets scientists stay in space for weeks at a time in a weightless laboratory. One astronaut stayed on board the old *Mir* space station for more than a year.

▼ The International Space Station runs on electricity provided by giant solar panels.

100 Human beings are amazing!

The biggest wonder of the world is you – a human being. You can think and act in ways no other animal – and no computer – can. We may never meet anything quite as amazing as ourselves in the whole of the rest of the Universe.

I DON'T BELIEVE IT!

Astronaut John Glenn was 77 when he went into space in 1998. He first travelled to space in 1962, 36 years earlier.

Index